Feminine to Female Gender Poems

Vashti Carrion

Presentation by *BookLeaf Publishing*

Web: www.bookleafpub.com

E-mail: info@bookleafpub.com

ISBN: 9789357696050

First edition 2023

DEDICATION

To my editors, Kirk Ramdath, Robin Barratt, Ana Stjelja, Ben List, Gauri Patil, Ellen Shriner, Kevin, Karen Taylor who believed in me and published my writing. I love you dearly.

Rose-Rosa Parks

There once was a Rose,
growing in a Park,
She was a bud,
This Rosa Parks in a park.
as petal by petal befell,
so did the civil rights movement,
when another petal fell
and they say
she said "no"
as shy as a rose--
was Rosa Parks who said no!

Frida "Free-dah" Kahlo

Frida Kahlo,
Whose name rhymes
With "free"
believed her feet
were bird wings,
Giving her brain
feathers and wings,
her paintings
were free
of fine lines,
shaved eyebrows,
and lip hair.
Her Unibrow
Was her universe.
Her Unibrow
was free of status quo
of eyebrows
needing to be groomed.
Free-da Frida Kahlo
is as free as her name,
rhyming with the word "free."

Sylvia Plath On Plath-form Heels

Sylvia Plath Platform
with her stardust platforms
from having reached the universe.
with her free-feet,
walking on open mic platforms---
a giant woman on platform heels,
she stomps to read
her poetry,
while wearing platforms,
that write, as she stomps,
the lyrical poetry
that confesses
her life's reality.
In stardusted platforms
millions of feet high---
that reached the sky,
In where her head
writes with the stars
and the stars whisper
of Earth's secrets.
And now,
Sylvia Plath in Platform heels,
takes a bow
on open mic platforms!

Edith Piaf Pea-af Restaurant

Edith Piaf Pea-af
who sings in French
to her friends
who are Friench!

Edith Piaf Pea-af
With a bowl of
pea soup
In her soul...

She sings,
"Je ne regrette rien"
and doesn't regret
her songs about peas
curing the ails
of -sickly-French-
restaurant-customers!
Music is curing for a soul!

Edith Piaf Pea-af
who sings with a soul,
her pea soups,
that come with a song
catering to the colds
of La France!

Do The Polka Pocahontas

Do The Polka Pocahontas,
In West Virginia
in Native American museums,
this dance, will make you muse:
to colonial times,
with one step in,
and one step out!
with Native Americans
and European unity:
When You
Do The Polka Pocahontas,
you all hold hands in unity!
See the race to a new race:
leaves racism to prehistoric times!
as you do,
Do The Polka Pocahontas!

L.M. Montgomery Didn't Shine

L.M. Montgomery,
Signed her books:
By L.M. Montgomery
and scholars of
Montgomery,
commented she wasn't
shining like the Dickens--
like Charles Dickens,
on a Christmas bulb.
because Canada's clouds
rained on scholar's brains
and fogged
L.M Montgomery's
feminine gender!
when she wrote Anne
of Green Gables
and wasn't shining like
the dickens! Or as Charles Dickens!

Louisa May-Day-Alcott

Louisa May Alcott
whose brain slept
in a cot,
when May Day celebrations
Commenced.
the brains
of writers from
New England
whose brain nested
on flower crowns
looking like bird nests
who took the query
of messenger birds.
and broke the hearts
of Laurie and Jo
Louisa May-Day-Alcott's
pen was lonesome,
of Love, as her heart was lonesome-ly alone,
likewise!

Plain-Jane Goodall

Plain-Jane Goodall
whose goodwill
took her from England
to Africa
where Gorillas
pound their hearts
and opened the
valves of their hearts
to the knowledge
of primates
and mating seasons,
and Jane Goodall's
love for primatology
was in a Gorilla's hand.

Sacagawea Birds

There once was a time
when once became Time,
leading a path the Indian
Sacawegea led Lewis and Clark.
leaving tiny Sacawegea birds,
by the footprints of explorers,
who kept her secrets--
Sacawegea's secrets,
of how her heart truly felt,
to guide these Europeans,
In-no-man-lands tread!

Even now, to this day,
If you hike slowly,
on the Lewis and Clark trail,
by the Pacific Northwest,
You might find a Sacagawea birds
who cry the wails of the indians
who lived when
no one owned America!

Finding Vivian Maier

Did you ask her feet?
They are blue-printed
with New York feet.
It's hard to find
Vivian Maier
Maybe you can find her,
In all the people
she's seen
within her camera-eye lens.
In a monochromatic
palette,
a reflection of a moment
that only she witnessed,
and preserved
by.
a.
shutter.
of.
a.
lens.
Spotted by the flutter
Of her eye-lens,
not just camera-lens.
Can you really find
Vivian Maier,
When she's not reflected
by her camera-lens.
You can ask a photograph

Or two,
"Where's Vivian Maier?
She not hiding,
behind her lens, is she?"
One photograph told me:
"She's not quite there
or you would stare,
in the composition
quite squared,"
directing me into
It's neighbor Image,
In a garland of
Vivian Maier images,
Pinned in a bulletin-board.
"where's Vivian Maier?"
I inquired to the dear printed
photograph.
"In the expressive expression
Of figures, two"
Another photograph intercepted:
"Or in the fumes of a cigarette
Laidback with finesse"
Or another photograph
spoke to me,
"you can find,
Vivian Maier,
In loving-lovers embraces"
within her copyrighted
Imagery.

Literary Female Figure: Mary Poppins Pimple

Mary Poppins Pimple,
Lives in Super-CALI-Frappuccino
a city in ol' foggy London,
donning her 1950's hat,
serving a bountiful bouquet,
the adorning
flowers of a tiny red hat!
that sing the gloomy songs,
Of ol' London autumn fogs.
Mary Poppins Pimple,
Cladded in a minty fresh dress
Like the airs of London's
lawning lawns.
grows a pimple
like pumpernickel
and inside the pimple
Grows a garden
the size of a nickel
and there goes
Mary Poppins Pimple,
With a garden in her pimple!

Amelia Ear-heart

Can you hear me,
Amelia Ear-heart,
with your humongous
ear,
what shall I ask,
if you will,
if you carry
a compass
for a heart,
how can you,
have ended
at Lost And Found Island
with a GPS
in the middle of
know where,
the first lady of the sky,
flying the
the seven skies.
Amelia Ear-Heart
can you hear me,
with your humongous
ear,
What shall I ask,
if you will,
if you carry

a compass
for a heart,
if your can re-route it,
to an Island Where I Am Found,
where I don't mind your,
humongous ear,
where you'll hear all
you've wanted to hear.
including a melody
composed by a blue-sky,
and cotton-cloud flowers,
for the First Lady of the Sky.

Georgia O'Keeffe's Sunsets

Georgia O'Keeffe
is a sunset-maker
of New Mexico, USA
She makes the world
Go to sleep
and dream of Paint.
with a painting palette
and the sky for a canvas,
she paints beyond the cacti,
blue scintillating hues,
that marry to iridescent
yellows—
that carry phosphorescent
red, bleeding into the evening, purple.
when the world is late-night-dark-in color,
her paintings carry the legacy of
Paint.
and sunset colors!
I have a piece of the sunset when the sun
is gone, by Georgia O'Keeffe paintings.

Feminine Landmarks: The Painted Ladies

Painted Ladies
in San Francisco,
historical homes
for visiting tourist,
as Mrs. Day
retires for a night,
the ladies
prepare for
a ladies night.
the windows open
with eyes
and mascara
hold them upright,
with Russian Red
lipstick-lips
and a pair of
old-fashion heels,
stemming from
a wooden floor
turn into a dancing floor,
the ladies can't wait
to come alive.
The Seven Sisters
as they say,

there's no fighting
for the fame,
whose "the fairest
home of them all",
with a clip'd purse
fill with cosmetics,
the seven ladies,
showcasing
femininity,
there's no shame
in Painted Ladies,
a home,
for femininity.
a Landmark with a female gender!

Twiggy--London Model

Twiggy,
and her flower power
eye,
Eye, with Peace and Love
that bursts into
Flower Power
landing on a Volkswagen
with petals,
Petals
that trail the Freedom
of groovy moves,
With larger purpose
from a flash of a camera
Twiggy, a London Model, with
A fashion statement:
That promotes world peace!

For Coco Chanel

Coco Chanel
Sewed female
and male social mores
together,
Creating darts
on menswear,
and sewing the iconoclastic
to French Fashion history.
with a drop of a red lipstick
by the Eiffel Tower,
leaving a red lipstick stain,
like a snail's trail...
Coco Chanel's red lipstick,
smears the plain out of
France's countryside,
Coco Chanel's red lipstick
is as bold as women's rights
dabs of red on a path
to equality,
this red Chanel lipstick
smudges
the self worth
of a human female
and the tender feelings
of being a woman.

Marie Antoinette's Cake Recipe

1 teaspoon of a wig
2 cups of egg sarcasm
1 flour of her Garden's flowers
300 milligrams of a fine gown
1 ½ of a wine glass

1. Marie Antoinette poured all the contents, 1 flour
of her Garden's flower
Into the bowl of the French Revolution, the sarcastic
egg ingredients fell on the French populace
poor heads! They have all been egged!
2. The teaspoon of a wig fell among the riots,
as the ingredients in the baking pan held together
by the 1 ½ glass of wine, making the batter refined!
3. As the cake baked,
and the 300 milligrams of a fine gown arose,
The censorship made her say
"Let Them Eat Cake" at the End!

Mother Teresa, From Mother Earth

Mother Teresa cared
 about Mother Earth,
The sentient sentiments buried in sediments,
In Mother Earth
Mother Teresa, so noteworthy and discovered.
Her "small acts of kindness" that surpass
average human
Act within the shovel of human life.
 by The Nobel Prize committee,
making earth blossom into noble yarrows
healing our humanity,
Of inhumanity!
Mother Teresa, From Mother Earth

Audrey Hepburn's Little Black dress

Audrey Hepburn's Little Black Dress,
mourns the extravaganza,
The black threads that hug the waist,
Of a woman,
Each stitch, is a simple statement,
a black pearl necklace
that laces and defines and creates simplicity
While the stars strike the guitar strings,
"Moon river" by the balcony,
Of an everyday woman,
With a life.
The music notes are on the rudimentary scales,
spotlighting
the aspects of living life as a woman!

Ellen Ochoa– Latina With Stars

Her pores breath stardust,
Left by her space explorations,
Ellen Ochoa reached the stars
And the human renditions
Of Stars as Christmas Tree Toppers,
The glitter
That emulates outer space, but doesn't burn
On planet earth.
This knowledge doesn't harm the environment:
Ellen Ochoa reached the stars
In gender-neutral pink!

Literary Female Figure: Juliet Capulet

Juliet And Her Balcony Romeos!
Sensing your sensations,
make a grand appearance!
To my fair Verona Plaza!
In where her
meatball microphone,
Wave Tsunami-ing
Italian ears:
Singing sonnets
Of swooning love
Right into Venezian ears!
Juliet And Her Balcony Romeos!
a breaking sensation,
and be sure your heart
Isn't broken
by her background dancers
The Balcony Romeos!
From Juliet,
singing love's tune!
A love labor's not lost!

www.ingramcontent.com/pod-product-compliance
Lightning Source LLC
LaVergne TN
LVHW021348200726
843509LV00014B/2734